With Such Caution

A Life Glimpsed in Short Pieces

Wendy Robertson

To Lynda

THIS WORK IS DEDICATED TO

Bryan, Debora, Grahame and Angus Robertson,
unique companions on a lifetime's journey.

Also Avril Joy, who showed me the poet's path
and walked along beside me in the year it took
to assemble this collection.

And to Dr. Donna Maynard, who unearthed many
of these pieces while researching my lifelong writing
notebooks and suggested that I should
collect them together in this form.

And crucially to the astute Gillian Wales, the
literary librarian with an eagle eye for words.

With so many thanks
love
Wendy Robertson.

Author's Note

I have gathered together here most of the short line pieces I have written in the last 50 years or so. Originally I called these *short line pieces* because they were just that to me. Unlike my other writing they are not short stories, although they have about them elements of the short story; neither are they novels, although in each one there is the potential, the essence of a novel.

It was some time before a literary friend took me to one side and told me these were really *poems*. So in recent years I have called them poems. Each one stands alone to be read on its own and be interpreted as it stands.

Anyway, these poems are pure glimpses of a life - some of them remembered 30 or 40 years later; some of them were written on the cusp of the events that inspired them to be revisited and re-interpreted as the years unfolded.

You will notice that the poems are not set out here in autobiographical time. Rather they are inspired by my feelings about them in the present ,as I edit them and put them in order for this collection. Perhaps the ordering constitutes a glimpse of my state of mind in the present day while I have been assembling this collection.

You will also note that the pieces vary widely in theme and content. Some poems carry footnotes to clarify the source of the inspiration for that poem.

Wendy Robertson
Bishop Auckland 2021

CONTENTS

DEDICATIONS
AUTHOR'S NOTE

Poems and Pieces 1962 - 2020

Outsiderness

Being the third child of four
I was bred to be an outsider.
Being the new child from a far town
I was labelled outsider.
Talking with the wrong tone
I sounded like an outsider.
Being the cleverest child in class
made me an outsider. Then,
working alongside men
I became a female outsider.
Telling stories has made me
always a mendacious outsider.
Living with a man who doesn't see
I am an intimate outsider.
Living through to old age
I am the ultimate outsider - relishing
this one thing - this Outsiderness.

A Time for Naming.

The third of four children,
she slipped out, barely noticed
among the dogs of war
and other fine distractions.
Later on she made you tea,
passed hard examinations -
and wrote so many books
just to warm your heart
and catch your eye.

She loved your story
- yourself as heroine –
of walking to the church
waist-deep in snow,
the baby in your arms and
Billy's arm around you.
You had to be there
to expiate your own sin,
while endowing her with
a name invented by the man
who loved lost boys.

My mother returns again and again
in my writing

London Street

Noises invade me in this city

– the clack of voices from the bus stand,

the purring roar of cars, the growling rumble

of red buses, the crack of fireworks, the scream

of fire engines, the plaintive wail of police sirens.

Two boys ignite a rocket on land

recently razed for social housing.

In the café a small girl pores over a thick book.

On the other side of the glass a woman in

a red hijab flies along the street on a bicycle

London Nov 5 .02. Also 2020
I have always relished my role
as outsider in London and yet it being my city.

Beginning

To begin anything

you have to end the earlier things.

Birth is the end of gestation -

conception is the end of a love affair

and the beginning of mother love.

We can go back, back to Eve -

even that event involved the end

of Adam's rib-cage.

But listen! What consequences

there are of that excision.

28th December 02 Also 2020
This principle also applies to a poem,
a short story, or a novel. A

Sirens

They stand there, the sirens -
short hair, muscular demeanour -
bluff, pragmatic, family men
here on the wrong planet.
'Let us see your papers,' they say.

So much standing, waiting. It
suits those standing, watching types.
They challenge me, grinning, the Remegel
and Ventolyn in my brown leather bag,
I wonder why I left them there.

The steel wall parts -
exposing electronic doors
and bullet-proof screens, giving
 an illusion of security, a sense of
enclosure. All siren safety.

*I feel this recurring nightmare has its origins
in my reading as a child the newspaper accounts
of incidents in of World War 2.*

With Such Caution

In her early life, timid and shy,
she pre-empted risks by keeping
her horizons low and her head
down over her books.

Then she read that one could '*Pre-empt risks*
with a single cautious thought.' But risk means no
sky-flight of a ball, no freedom path of a kite,
and even worse - no stories written,

She found that with such caution
no loves would be loved, no fights fought,
no truths proved, no lies told and
no great journeys into far lands.

With such crippling caution
there would be no lives lived, and
regret would rule forever
on the walls of primitive caves.

> *My life has been one long adventure*
> *of overcoming my timidity,*

Hot Day

Above her trees seethe
and shake in the still sun
The snake heat crawls up
her brown arm. Alongside
her half-closed eye
the green hill reaches the sky,

The air, fried dry of moisture,
still retains a whisper of
its night-time drenching -
finally refusing to surrender
to the primal heat of
this late, great, sun.

The fading heat still scorches
her arms, her legs, investing
her heart and gut with visceral
pleasure. How good, she thinks,
that this impersonal passion
leaves no scars.

*A very early list which started life
in my local park when I was about fifteen.*

.

BA Market Square: A Writer's List

Rain slicks the blue van to a shine.
The market stalls have left their spoor -
water lies in pools on the town square.
Just a vague reflection of a bad day's takings.

At the last flower stall gleaming raindrops
press down on the bright cyclamens.
The trader crouches like a dealer, her
red hoody shadowing her bleak face.

Another woman - her bleached hair
hanging down like snakes - hauls
her son from school -
Like snails, they are both unwilling.

I feel there's something rather
rakish about that open blue umbrella.

'Start with a list!' I say to new writers.
Naked observation and noting down is the key.
This square has been a feature in my life for fifty years,
It's a writer's benefit to see it like a stranger.

Dawdon Colliery

Dirty cotton-wool sky
blotting up Prussian Blue
and Yellow Ochre -
cloaked in metal tubes
funnelling Monestial Blue to the sea,
while churning Flake White
and Mars Violet in the mix.

Scratched-in pebbles
glow there on the sand
blackened by years
of sluicing coal waste –
the profit from black gold
still lining pockets
unto the sixth generation

A pitman walks his thin dog here,
his daughter trails behind them.
But there, just off centre,
I can see another child
wearing a dress of Carmine -
blood or life, survival or death,
depending on the generation.

The truth that lies in the paintings of the gifted
Tom McGuinness has always been
an inspiration in my work.

The Pier

A family of striped chairs -
below the first pier, stork-legged
like a colliery gantry - is drawn up in a circle
like prairie schooners on the dingy sand.

The second pier is fragile - lurching
to the left on awkward legs - still bravely lit
by random splashes
of Titanium white,

In the right corner of the canvas
a man in a blue cap paddles
in the sun. My eye is drawn, left-centre
to a woman painted in Red Ochre.
Blood and hope reflected in
waves rippling behind her.

Inspired by another McGuinness painting.
His paintings tell their own story.
'First make a list!'

Them Thar Hills

'Is this cowboy country?' *
my older brother asks,

The pit heaps here
in this alien country create
rigid triangles against the sky.
The green stretching land
exposes the horny sharpness
of the slag - rejected now, after
the harvesting of the coal.
These days the soft beauty
of the rising land - in recovery from
the sterile heaps - is enriched
by trees feathering the sky,

This alien place is our heritage –
no longer cowboy country, son.

18ᵗʰ June 1966
*My older brother Tom actually said this*when,*
after our father died, our family came up
from Coventry to live in the North,

Different Worlds

Won't you please let her be her own self -
isolated, pedantic, fumbling, distrustful,
knowing, funny and even empathetic?
But that is not permitted in this world.

She must be a good girl. She must stay quiet .
She must neither speculate nor say what she thinks.
She must bite her tongue as she watches the stars
rise and make their pattern in the firmament.
She must stay silent as joy floods her being
at the sight of a child dancing and
suppress her unique perception of the years
passing through the millennia.

Meanwhile there is this other self with that pulsing
god in her head flushing her with power
and mindful complexity, even while she talks with
you of daytime triviality. And while she smells the
sodden leaves releasing the latent perfume of
summers past and bruising the air with feeling; she
may only talk of the change in the weather,
and can only say, *Oh yes, time does fly*.

Perhaps all writers develop such second selves.

Cathedral City

Hooded shapes march across the transept
transformed through time by faith's siren song.
Outside, the mass stone tower
Is relieved only by string-bead lights
as its bells signal the call to early vespers.

In the town beneath the holy church
the coiling streets hide obscure,
sacred places - untouched as yet by
young embraces - filled with shadows
yet only inhabited by black cats.

Vespers bells still boom away
spearing sound across the town,
past hiking shops and fast food places,
down green-treed banks to the young sports
who wield their oars to dominate the water.

On the riverside path she sees those
Same hooded figures in procession.

For many decades Durham City
has offered me a spiritual and
and inspirational escape

Billy: A Daughter's Tale

We walked along, your giant's hand in mine, long
fingers poking inside my hand-knitted sleeve.
Remember the nights she left the house for work?
You sat and read the paper as I scaled your knee
settling, birdlike, into that rustling space.

Remember how we cut out pictures
and pasted them into the Panjandrum book?
Remember how you read us stories -
your voice going up and down
like the waves of the sea?

So very sorry you don't know my youngest —
like you he's highly numerate - you
did not see him standing tall for Tai Kwan Do
(white clad and obliquely oriental)
or cricket-ready, complete with pads
and helmet and faceguard protection.

(Continued)

It's a lifetime since I passed your dying age
of thirty seven. And now I contemplate
how very young you were when
you abandoned your life and mine,
when - to my nine-year self - you seemed eternal.

It has taken two generations
between then and now for me
to ventilate the retrospective pain
of losing you too soon.

> *My father died when I was nine and I see now*
> *that - even without him - our relationship*
> *was the template for my eventual identity.*

A Marriage

This marriage went to work
and loved it; it wore flowers
 in its hair; and wore sober suits
 and hippy skirts; it walked
children in prams and pushchairs
and attended parents' meetings.

This marriage loved the seaside, keeping
warm in two hand-knitted Shetland ponchos.
This marriage went to the races, to rugby matches
and school plays; it waved children off to a
strange new life and welcomed them back again -
all changed and full of opinions.

This marriage watched cricket, football, TV News.
It consumed newspapers, read books, and
dared to write them. It attended clinics and hospitals
and held its breath. This marriage still misses the
clever boy
who loved chocolate and now lives and works
across a great ocean.

This is a marriage that still holds hands.

This one speaks very much for itself, I think.

Black Rain

As I step out on this wet spring morning
so many thoughts weigh me down.
Stepping on sods with this leaden core,
my mind is heavy; my body more so -
my feet have to haul this excess weight.

The sky looms above me, pressing down,
now, here is the sun, shining down!
Still my heavy footprint trace my way
on the sodden grass.

I feel sad that the snake-shine pathways
of my mind must perpetually unload
their dark bitterness on those around me.

May 21 1966
Battling with depression is a common writer's plight
walking hand in hand, as it does, with the
uncertainties of creativity.

Sea Mirror

No-one knows her, but she knows them.
For him she is the sea on the change - sometimes
glittering, storm-grey and surging. But also dark
and still - far too deep - yet sparkling, reflecting .
 She harbours light and shade.
and whispers music of the deep
before making love in sweet rushes.

How can anyone say they know her?
What people know is the side that pleases –
the most effective mirror of their own thoughts –
a familiar reflection of their own world-view –
an echo of their own instincts.
When you peer over the side of the boat
into calm water you will see yourself whole.

But she can throw in a stone
and you'll be split into fragments.
How can you say you know her?

*In my worst moments I feel that
all relationships are based on equal parts of
self-love and deception.*

Translucent Butter Muslin

I wake up trembling, time ringing, vibrating,
calling the angelus. In my dream I see you,
arms raised - backlit in translucent butter muslin.
You are a vision pulsing before me
Manufactured by the stars glimmering
in the sky at night. Now I see you smiling -.
my father stoops over you, his arm slung
around your plump shoulders.
Now I see you in a fluffy white coat,
your red hair blazing, waiting at my school-gate,
Now I see you in a blue crêpe party dress
toggled in amber.at the neck
Now I see you at my brother's wedding,
wearing a blue hat, its brim upturned.
Best of all - I see you standing up straight
- blue uniformed and silver-buckle-belted.
But here and now I see you standing
at the top of my stairs in translucent butter muslin
— your arms raised towards me.

*My gifted, clever, forceful mother Barbara persists in
my dreams and emerges in my stories as well
as the poems and short pieces here.*

The Wind from the Sierra

In the twilight of the ward
the old woman pulls me to her side
and whispers in the tight shell of my ear.
Her voice, dancing on a roaring tide,
surfs sixty years of life
with West Coast ease.
I let down my hair, she says, *when I
was nursing in the Spanish War.
After the lice, the blood, the mucus-mud
of that First Conflagration —
many women cut their hair,
silky smooth to their skulls.
Not me! I treasured my locks.
Daytime on the ward I wore my hair
tightly bound, moulded to my head
like a Roman helmet. And every night
I brushed it out, tress by golden tress -
a miserly Rapunzel alone in my room.*

Of course, I say, since that Spanish prelude
haven't we had our own wars here?
Not so much the innocence of fighting
face-to-face, toe to toe, but cities raped,
skies riven, fire storms raging.

(Continued.)

How does this compare with
the cloth-capped Spanish anarchy - all fluttering
flags and posters - pitted innocently against
the tyranny of flying steel? Later generations
paid world-rates for learnéd arguments
and justification – from comfort-men in suits.
Little comfort, though, for hearts ripped
out of cities and of citizens, when the price
of planes and bombs was paid in flesh and pain,
and administered by medallioned clerks.

In the twilight of the ward the voice in my ear
is now a fading tide smelling of salt and iodine,
of Dettol and of rotting fish.
I liked to feel it lifting,
in the warm wind from the Sierra.

While researching my grandson's Spanish heritage
I came across an old woman who, as a girl, had
nursed fighters in the Spanish Civil War.

Trees

Green light drips onto sooty bark -
and the white sun forges pathways
onto yellow aconite petals,
spotlighting chunky bluebells
awakened from their ancient bulbs.

Raw branches push outwards and up
Straining to escape their broad trunk -
a descendent of the ancient woodland
rooted here, predating the existence of
 the Main Street, even the whole town.

In later times a crude, straight street echoes
with the tramp-tramp of mercenary feet
pacing the land, holding it in thrall
for an emperor lounging now
 in glimmering Mediterranean light.

Now this child walks through the trees,
trailing her plump hand on the roughened bark.
She puts her face up to the sky and savours
the pearls of rain that drop onto her round
brow into her closed eye.

*Found in a 2002 notebook. I worked on it during the 2020-21
Lockdown which I've spent at my desk in the bay window
looking out on my trees of ancient heritage which
have been my familiars during this dry period.*

Easter Sunday in Romaldkirk

I brought a picnic -
cheese and jam sandwiches,
a pear ripened in the window -.
and the red flask, normally for rugby.

Visitors park their cars here
and promenade around the green -
older couples welded to a single form,
a grandmother with a baby in a stroller,
a family with children - the father stout,
wearing a belly-tight Newcastle strip.
I notice two ladies, (all Country Casual'd
Their heads swathed in silk scarves),
and a young couple leaping from
a silver-blue sports car.

My eye fixes on ghosts - more demure in dress —
who join the promenade. For them
'Sunday Best' is a good change
from workaday clothes. They relish
the feeling of Being Decent
on a good Sunday

These old trees are eternal watchers
around this village green, with
its ancient church in one corner
and its stylish pub at its centre.

For many years I liked to escape alone on Sunday,
making lists to pin down my first impressions.

A Dream

There is a window, sharp, grey-edged,
fixed in a wall, crossed at the centre
like the sign of Jesus. Through the
misted window I see a white cloud forming -
the gentle shape of a mushroom in the air.

I stand there, watching - rigid as a bar of iron -
as the white heat melts the window glass.
I try to reach out for my children,
but - being too slow - I cannot even
hold my children as we die.

Being born early in World War 2. my growing years
were engulfed with a sense of catastrophe
that embedded itself in my soul and printed itself on my mind.

A Time for Burning

I stand staring at the harvest -
corn, rolled thick and tight on
pillaged stubble in
such a random fashion.
These rolls of corn have in them
so many hours of sunshine, tides of rain
with gales of wind. And, from time to time,
they have been touched by the odd rainbow

But now it is the end of season –
and for the stubble it is
a time for the burning.

The rhythm of the year in the rural landscape
that surrounds my town illuminates my perception
of the world in equal measure with the old houses
and streets, in my town and the
older trees that define it.

Schooling

Chubby children dance through the gates,
filled tight with cornflakes and bread and jam.
This boy comes from a beetle-browed building
with aerials sprouting from its summit.
Its paramilitary windows are surrounded by
high walls still topped by iron railings.
Stains drip down the concrete like spilled icing,
walkways open to a thousand neighbours and
bright washing turns black again in two days.
Now the boy dances through the double doors
and here comes a thin girl - all angles -
side-stepping inside the shadow of the high wall.
Once inside, she spends her school day
in one overstuffed room, littered and lined
with learning from other years.
Here she learns to quench her spring,
to obey the wise around her and accept the over-
peopled building: all part of A Great Pattern,
furnishing her with borrowed wisdom
tempered by the gift of suffering?

A teacher steps out of her car, stands up straight,
and sets out briskly to face her day.

This piece encompasses my experience of education both as a pupil
and teacher. The combination of dread and opportunity ride
shotgun on an individual's experience of schooling.

Apple Tree.

The tree blossoms in the yard

its root feet breaking though the concrete -

imploding with tender strength. Its ragged stick-like

branches cut back now back to ugliness

by a loving hand - only to ensure

that first the blossom,

then the fruit, will emerge.

1966

This fragment from an early notebook finds place
here because it reminds me of the backyard
of that tiny house where I spent my growing
years and shows the power of the natural
world even in the most deprived setting.

The Horse Breaker

I tramp across the field, at the side
of the man who breaks horses.
No wind, but my face is freshening -
the day is cold but still my features burn.
A bird rises up - its wings beat the air.

A horse snickers and canters across -
steam rising from its broad back.
Its coat sports a rank shine;
its mouth glitters with old sores -
ancient scores, still not settled

And here is the man; his clanking boots
stamp tender clover underfoot - he grasps
a woven leather whip in his wiry brown hand.
His weathered face glows and his hard
black eyes glitter, ready for the morning's work.

(Continued)

Later on, we will walk through his fields -
beat his boundaries and check his fences.
He will show me the ruins of antique houses -
their stones now tumbled - built by
members of his ancient family.

Two birds rise in feral combat,
fluting and fluttering -
a dispute with no resolution.

An unforgettable encounter on a family holiday
on a Scottish farm. I came away tingling
with awareness of many diverse emotions.

Cher Ami

Iron grey stone lumped against the sky
looming over the tide, its imposing
corduroy swirls on the sand -
carving, forming, manufacturing
unexpected shapes in my brain.

A fairy ring etched into the grass
induces magic myth, even if with
scientific explanation. These
silver rings glitter in pale sunshine
lit by luminous interior light

But there are softer scenes in my head
looping, holding, seeking, investing
the sea with colour – and I retain them all,
branding them right there into my brain.

Codified disclosure, perhaps.

Tin Drum Beat

Lady of shadow, where do you walk?
Come into the light
let me see you more clearly,
Grasping existence with your metal fingers
Sitting there hearthside to knit up the world
your face set hard to the distance of time,
your green-coin head turns this way and that,
viewing the treeless spread of the city.
Still you stay there at the edge of the dark
walking the streets with your diamond tread
beating the drum with your tough metal fingers -
choosing the child for the next conflagration.

Lady of shadow, where are you walking?
Come into the light
Let me see you more clearly
You turn into an alley, darker than Hades,
and confront a boy whose eyes cannot see.
Your gaze pierces through the husk of his eyelid
igniting his soul to the darkness ahead,

Lady of shadows
Come into the light
Let me see you more clearly

(Continued)

I'm running before you, afraid of your gaze
afraid of your hands with their tin-drum-beat
afraid of your eyes, those glittering emeralds,
afraid of the high-heeled click of your feet

Lady of shadows why do you follow?
I turn in the dark to meet your embrace.

Nov 29.02
Fragments of this poem are in several of the
notebooks. Perhaps this piece shows how
close are one's dreams and nightmares
in a world where the imagination rules.

Snow

Peering through steamed-up windows
I see snow now, pressing on the trees
in my garden and steering
down the outside panes in soft runs.

Outside, each sound is dimmed -
a shriek is lost, becomes a whisper,
a crash floats across the silence,
the birds forget to sing.

The white blanket makes colours fade.
Even red becomes black, the trees are
dark lace and children
are transformed to darting shadows.

Snow hangs upon the world
heaving itself onto the waiting fields,
while cars coming and going on the old road
leave their traces in sleazy white lines.

Watching snow during Lockdown
intensifies the focus,

33

Three Thirty a.m.

Your name dances through
my brain - projecting outwards.
to be read on my skin.
Virtue certainly takes effort
and condemns feelings into a
deep freeze. Getting things
into proportion is to pretend
they don't exist. Still
the ache for you buzzes
like a bee in my limbic system.
The thing is, without you my brain
is only half alive - even though
you are only marginally there.

All lives truly lived have their secrets,

The Marauder

I climb dark steps of old stone,
a door broken into the wall -
with barbed wire and shards of glass
on its summit to keep marauders out.

But now the house is laid wide open as -
pierced by a single look, a single word -
the wall melts. Barbed wire melts
to silver cord and shards of glass
are transformed into diamonds.

The marauder strides in
exploring the special rooms
and the secret places
before - his face in shadow -
retreating backwards.

Another bad dream from a post war childhood..

Oh Boudicca!

Your hair is the colour of a bright penny
much admired by everyone.
 Mam - also red-haired - says,
Just like Boudicca and the first Elizabeth -
great women, both.

At first you wear your hair in long plaits
hooked up with green ribbons. One day
I sit on the stairs listening to the two of them
shout – school is looming as she insists
on cutting off those long plaits;

My own hair – curly and tangled, mostly unkempt -
means that I'm christened Medusa by cruel boys
at school, where clever does not count and where
I'm never picked for teams and am ignored
by you in corridors. Unhappy times.

And then each day, with my tangled hair and
slipshod ways, I walk ten paces behind you.
on our long walk to school.
You do not turn and as for me
for certain I am entirely alone..

Continued

But with your clever mind and bright-penny hair
you take your place among the racy girls
who admire your dancing style and love
those green shoes with four-inch heels –
that Mam has bought for you on credit .

At school your friends - too cool to study –
hold you back, drag you down,
and stop you showing your clever brain.
But then you surge on in the world
and rise to the top with relative ease.

Remembering Susan,
my charismatic, clever sister,

Boundaries

Shining edges mark the tired green
and shadows stretch right to the house.

Me, I'm old as the darkest corner,
never content I am restless in the gut -
restless although happy still
knowing I am still alive.
I know people who are dead
while living – walking, sitting, making love –
but *happy!* They would say.
I know so much about substantial joy
and I am fully acquainted with
isolation, distance, unfamiliarity,
but have no regret for the nonconformity
that first gave me the courage to feel the joy,
the courage to embrace the isolation
and welcome the humility of total feeling.
Is it better, though, to relish feeling uninvolved?

The silver edges are fragment on the grass
I move bare feet in soft blades
itching with fresh feeling.

I spend much of my life in a state
of such confusion.

A Fine Romance

I hope you like roses. *I get lots of roses*
I am sure you do. You must have many admirers.
I do - men are fools. Do you despise men?
Only certain men, who show themselves wanting.
You seem to be a very testing companion
They tell me so. Do you like nothing about me?
I like your boots. They are the finest boots,
made by craftsmen. *And your whip!.*
It looks very fine. Here! You may have it.
You strip yourself of power! I would do anything
to win your favour. *That would never happen.*
You're too lightheaded - in my view.

*Ah! Relationships! There is something comic about
Such encounters,*

Doctors

Small, neat, good skin -
sweet smile, soft hands
engendering confidence.

Fine fingers prodding -
voice low and reassuring.
It will go. It will go.

She shows me how
to open my mouth with spatulas.
In fear, I fold my lips tight.

Then I see another doctor and
the world explodes in my face.
He makes a hole, drains off the poison.

A Professor (or some such)
stands before me, all waistcoat and braces
round pudding face and brisk moustache.

He fingers his chin and says.
'People die of this, you know!'

Clinical treatment for severe jaw infection.
Excruciationg.

Unforgiveable

It's so wrong to wander here
viewing you as objects
even while feeling
intensely benevolent .

Am I using you
to indict a brutal system?
Am I casting you in the role
of slaughtered lamb?

Am I making you
a savage symbol
of my own dark side?
I forget that at my peril.

Do I make you into vessels
of my insecurity, frail
conscience keepers
of my dark side?

Reflecting on my experience in prison –
a life-changing and life-enhancing experience,.

Stone Circle

The stone ring seems natural -
brought into being by the *chip-chipping*
of a man with strong fingers.
It's not quite regular, perhaps
his twine and measuring stick only
served for a rough and ready job.

Still, his stone circle is fit for purpose -
for the cluster of rock dwellers
gathering at the moon rising
to tell their stories and
exchange their goods, relishing
the profit from their surplus.

They sit there, in the circle
snug atop the plateau, dead centre
of the low surrounding hills,
like the sun and its puny planets.

When I am in an ancient places
I often have the sense of seeing through time
It can be quite intimidating

Birds

The line of birds scratches its way

across the smoky grey blanket -

of this January afternoon,

its random form

finally establishing

an elegant double Vee.

The birds flap their way North

obeying an urgent inner tick

to escape the sultry fog

the warmth and the opulent

surge of spring bulbs making

their way into the light.

Birds and squirrels are the only wild things I see
in everyday domestic life.

Blue Jaguar

Her ears crackle and she holds her breath
as churches, houses, halls and corner shops
canter by at such a pace.
She sees her own end mirrored
in a smaller windows -
one pane even shows a mangled death.

In a larger window clusters of figures
crowd in quiet corridors - people talking,
some even lifting their heads in laughter,
At last she sees the stony steeple -
her true birth-right – showing
she was here once and will be again.

Now - a comic strip unreeling -
the land flows past bright reaching corn
as the Jaguar purrs by, eating up the miles.

Her body, not understanding,
opens up. It flowers
in involuntary exhilaration.

Cars are often the source of surreal experiences for me.
This is a journey to Scotland in a Jaguar – a car
Which was the achievement of an ambition

Dark

Slate grey gauze drawn across,
old hands put together with dry care.
New smooth hands placed on top -
held firm in young hands -
smooth and turned in slightly.

Strange shadows surge across the sky -
two people linked together, joined by
 broad hands, knowing nicely
what each other has known
and relishing it.

White buildings rise up, scar-like on
the road, illuminated as the grey veil lifts
above the jagged line of roofs -
all familiar now. How sweet to discover
that good people survive.

A dream or a nightmare. Perhaps both,

Paradox

She wants to be alone, not to feel
their searching eye, their reaching hands,
their small fingers that appear
to be grabbing the air but in truth
they grasp her very core.

She shrinks away from beguiling
conversations, from high-pitched voices ,
from empty plates upon the table -
from the oven standing there -
she only wants to be alone.
But involuntarily she cultivates this deep desire -
to reach out for their reaching hands,
and shout into their urgent ears.
In the end she can't endure
her self-chosen isolation.

So she reaches out to hold them,
to touch their skin, to stroke their faces
to kiss their cheeks. She surrenders now -
conscious that she needs them, and should
cast off her wilful separation.

*The paradox and pleasure of motherhood for
the undomesticated,*

The Veil

She fears the power of her own mind
after a lifetime spent disguising the strength
and the passion of genuine feeling
which outweighs the negative force of anti-feeling -
her life spent behind the veil with a personaility
never fully expressed as she searches
for social acceptance.

Perhaps we all create the lie that we live by.

Knowing You

I am conscious of you -
my eyes, my skin, my very flesh -
they all know you. The walls recede,
the books dance off the shelves -
red and blue break down to fine dots,
bright molecules of colour, sharp
and cruelly definite, then they dissolve
into a holistic sensuality.

Daylight burns atom-bright
through the narrow window
onto a bolt of cloth whose shining
parallels stream on forever.
The music gets under my skin
demanding movement. The notes
separate, hold, and hang in the air
like … suspended … rain.

I know you and now I know myself.
You laugh and I turn my head.

The strongest emotions sometimes slip through the veil.

A Thousand Year Old Poem

We are parting

at the time when the leaves

are withered and keep on falling.

The cutting winds of autumn

batter my heart,

bringing sorrow to every part

of my mind and my body

making me die inside.

Now, all I have to cherish

are our bygone times, our old days.

Oh! In what time of our lives

in what part of the world

could you and I ever meet again?

Written In prison – a collaborative translation with Xiaocsa He –
a remarkable young woman.. Included here because
my prison experience was life-changing.

Wounds

I am invaded by
an overwhelming urge
to apologise for our trivial lives,
no dead bodies, just
bruises of vanity,
wounds of incontinence,
and pressures of inadequacy.
Continuing existence
implies a cult of mediocrity.
.

No war, no wounded,
no wondrous cause.

> *Widespread media exposure brings visions of pain and suffering*
> *to the corner of our living rooms, onto our desks and,*
> *into our lives, This exposure induces feelings of anger*
> *guilt and helplessness.*

Dream of Barbara

She is in the new place now, sitting there in a
high back chair - bones less brittle, flesh
now blooming, brown eyes piercing.

In that place, finding her lack of faith
disproved she returns now to her best self -
a fierce young woman with all before her.
She was much loved then, despite having
a red-haired temper which could induce
fear and compliance. Now, she recognizes
the critical view I was driven to take
in order to survive. Sorting things out
with her was too hard — a path to self-destruction,

Now, in the chair, she says, '*You are forgiven, pet.
Maybe you can do some forgiving too.*'

> *My mother yet again. Although dead for decades
> she is always there by my side, at my shoulder.*

Hysteria

On the loss of the first cradle -
no fixing of a broken leg
no skin graft on an injured hand -
this treatment excises a person's core.
It is no trivial loss.

My wedding rings – one wide, one narrow-
are blandly veiled with masking tape.
'Magnetism and machinery
can be a problem, you know!'
For fifty years this narrow ring sat on
my mother's finger. The wider ring is mine.
(I took it off for years, for ideological reasons.
And then I put it on again)
My mother's ring was still on her finger
as she was shunted on a trolley - mouth
set tight, swallowing fear, resenting the
patronage of her own profession.   (Continued)

To them she's just another old woman.
But she wants to shout, to show them
her younger self, apron crisply starched, the
silver-buckled belt clinching her waist. (Continued)

(

Justice would be served if I died here too-
a proper fate for a failing daughter
who let her mother slip away like that,
without anticipating her ending.

Now my mouth shuts tight as I fight the panic -
distilled over anxious months -
at the seriousness of this action
which will remove my mother-self.

The Dalek-hum of trolley wheels -
a brisk voice purring, *Nail polish?*
False teeth? Jewellery? Chemicals?
Magnets? They can cause trouble you know!

.

Let's get them off! There's enough
trouble in here already. Metal clinks in the tray.
And the stench of bleach and Savlon fills
my section of the ward.

And now I'm feeling sad, despite
this nurse in blue with the clinched-in waist.
This child-faced girl with her soft hand in mine
is the same age as my daughter, now abroad.

The trolley skims along under white lights
I know. The girl in blue pats my arm. (Continued)

People are afraid. All of them
Me, I would be the same

Now faces loom around my head,
nodding just like ears of corn,
saying things I can't make out
in their dreamy, fading voices.

Later harsh intonations boomerang
against the walls of the recovery room
calling me by name - *Wendy! Wendy!* -
time, and time and time again.

My teeth have been clamped too long
around this rubber breathing tube.
She won't do it. Open! open
your mouth, dear. Come on now!
The next day I'm on the ward,
feeling safe, propped up on pillows
in a high white bed. My throat is sore-
I can say no words.

This is no fixing of a broken leg
no skin-graft on a broken hand.
This is a final rite of passage —the removal
of my daughter's first bloody cradle.

I have long thought that the term hysterectomy is too cold a term for this process.

Languedoc

I keep taking these
sleight-of-hand photos
of the narrow alleys and big doorways.
I know that the pattern of some streets here
rolls back nearly three thousand years
The tall buildings huddle together to keep
the shaded streets cooler in summer,
turning their backs on seaborne storms in winter.
The tall, narrow houses are decieving -
behind the doors are courtyards, interior gardens,
warrens of rooms and sky-high staircases
The centre houses here were once called *islands*.
Our house is on the *Isle de Barry* -
once the domain of some lordly soul —
which is now divided into many dwellings. These
grand dwelling-places with massive arches and
peeling doors exited in earlier incarnations.
And these battered, peeling exteriors
disguise the still surviving grace and style
of the dwelling places within.

> *The Languedoc — an ancient place where I feel I've*
> *walked for a thousand years - proved to be*
> *the inspiration for several novels.*

Tree Sisters

In my garden three lanky sisters stand
side-by-side elbow-to-elbow, nodding their heads
and gently touching each other,
with fluttering fingers and knobbly elbows,
savouring the ever-present chime of birdsong.

Their ancient tree-brothers, high as my house,
stride our steep bank. Tangled up
and overgrown, their thick trunks are
embroidered with wild, wandering creepers.
unimpeded by the fecund ivy.

I leave the three sisters with their luminous trunks
and climb down the bank, ankle-deep in the
ancient leaf-skeletons, on a path
that winds its way down through
the thick trunks of grandfather trees.

And now an iridescent blue sparks through
the veil of filtered sunlight, as bluebells,
spawned by ancient bulbs, blunt-nose
their way between the roots of their foster fathers,
these ancient colonising trees.

Observed and observing me through my writing room window.

On My Mind

My mind - you have been on it all day -

behind the steady pattern of my tasks

watching me creaming soup for the supper,

hearing my voice rehearse the great lecture

catching my glance as I read the next chapter

driving beside me, moving into top gear,

Of course I want you there as

I sense you through my skin and my flesh

into my heart and right into my mind.

Clearly I love you with my whole self.

All this love fills me with complex joy.

And, paradoxically, brings with it

a certain sadness.

A subtle and most complete relationship.

A Death

A casual meeting,
a pleasant evening contact -
we talked like old friends.
(I was charmed by your smile.)
Touched by your flattering consideration -
although you made me feel my age –
so young and full of promise, as you
bustle about, business-like, but still a boy

Now I feel a pain.
A most attached sorrow.
As though I'd known you well.
As though we'd been close
since childhood.

I have a feeling that this one speaks for itself,

White Silk Tassels

Don't they open their eyes wide??
Their teeth bite, bite like lions —
their soft hands, smooth-pussy paws —
going for the cream with tongues of sandpaper:
My friend Kath sits dreaming on the bedspread
whose white silk tassels hang down to the floor.

Kath's aunt and uncle both have red faces —
his more bulbous, hers pale and sharp as razors.
I notice the two of them watching when
I go there to play with Kath in the bedroom,
with the white silk bedspread. She is three years
older than me but is still my very best friend.

As time goes by the white silk tassels vanish
one by one. Her eyes wide open, Kath tells me
that she plays this game with her uncle.
She says he says the white silk tassels
have been bitten off, most probably
by Cookie, their pet cat.   (Continued)

At breakfast Kath's auntie piles butter on her toast.
Their house - Jerry-built like our own —
is three doors down and, like our own,
is fenced with chicken wire.
But - unlike us - they don't have chickens. (Continued)

59

My Daddy - prone to mistakes – went out
and bought a dozen chicks for breakfast eggs.
His ring, swinging above their fluffy heads,
goes to the left. So we learn that these
fluffy birds are cocks, every one.
Mammy says, *No chucky eggs for us, love!*

Still, Kath a*M*nd I get praise for feeding these boys
and cleaning their cage, made from chicken wire.
We watch them leap and try to fly
and talk to them in chicken language,
all the time clucking over them like mothers.
  Kath tells me, then, that her mother died in Ireland.
(Continued)
Come Christmas, their little necks must be wrung -
not a job for Daddy – who has a soft heart.
But I watch my uncle smile as his strong fingers
squeeze out of their little chicken lives.
His shining red face, reminds me of Kath's uncle,
when he calls her in for tea.

That same Christmas my friend Kath takes
her Post Office savings, and runs away to London..
Her auntie burns the bedspread in the garden
Sure, our Kath's a sly cat – bad to the core and so ungrateful
. And we all watch as a burning tassel
shrivels on the chicken wire.

The realities of an innocent childhood friendship where the realities
of incest are beyond the child's vision.

Harem, Scar'em : The Road North,

Two hours travelling in massive pain -
with painkillers, cigarettes, cups of coffee.
Two hours - keep going, keep going.
Two hours - keep going, keep going
Two hours - keep going, keep going.

No point in speaking -
focus on the road, the road.
And now we can breathe out,
The sign says it all -
The North .

An emergency race to safety with
my best friend – the compass
set to Due North

Languedoc Marketplace: Mme Patrice

On my table *vin rosé* glitters
in a long stemmed glass. I smell coffee
and bruising fruit, and watch as
a burly man stacks cheeses on his stall -
placing them neatly, like books on a shelf.
His moving shadow is etched in
the bright light of the Languedocean midday.
A thin man moves through the stalls,
a load of vine stems on his back , and
a thin girl weaves her way through the café.

At a table near me a silver-haired woman
sits straight-backed, a small dog at her feet.
She meets my eye. A smile of recognition
lights her face. 'I'm called Madame Patrice,'
she says. 'I was just fourteen --when I was –
how do you say? A *courier* in the Resistance.'

I nod my head, smile, and say,
 "Will you walk into my story?'

*From the moment I arrived in this glorious part of France I realised that I'd
known it in other times. This short piece emerges from the notebook that ended
up as my novel. "An Englishwoman in France',whose heroine, Starr,* **has**
*second sight. In this – as you will see from other pieces here –
it reflects my own experience of seeing through time*

Ink, Blood, and Notebooks

Words flow from her heart into her brain.
Her brown pen drinks its fill from
a round pot filled with ink as black
as the darkest night. She feels the
blood flow from her brain, then
course down her arm and melt into
the black ink in her brown pen
before spelling out the words
 on the blank page in her notebook.

Notebooks, large, small and medium-sized -
filled with 50 years of inky sprawl –
march along the shelves in her writing room.

On her table sits a new red book -
just wating, open at a blank page.

I tell new writers that using free-flowing pen and ink
is the only way to embark on any writing..
Computers have their later uses but
this is the only way to begin.

The Author

After spending half of her working life teaching and training teachers as well as writing a weekly column for the Northern Echo Wendy Robertson became a full time writer.

Since then she has published more than 20 works of historical fiction as well as short story collections of her own and students' work as well as various articles. She has also mentored other writers and run a series of workshops on a wide range of themes associated with writing – most recently focusing on memoir.

This collection in many ways reflects that growing interest in the nature of memoir and how it emerges through different forms of writing.

She has a well followed blog full of essays and thoughts about her writer's world

http://lifetwicetasted.blogspot.com/

As well this she has an occasional website associated with broader aspects of reading, writing and self-publishing.

https://damselflybooks.com/

Contact: wenrob73@hotmail.com

Publications.

These titles are in no particular order. You might check them for further details on Wendy Robertson's blog
http://lifetwicetasted.blogspot.com/
or go to her Amazon Author page at
http://tiny.cc/kp9ctz

Kaleidoscope: *Short Story Collection*
The Romancer: *About Writing.*
Pauley's Web: *Prison life.*
Becoming Alice: *A strange child in London and Newcastle.*
The Bad Child: *A child chooses not to speak,*
An Englishwoman in France: *A woman who sees through time.*
Writing at the Maison Bleue: *Six very different writers on retreat,*
No Rest for the Wicked *(A take on Theatre life.)*
A Woman Scorned *(An alleged female serial killer.)*
Cruelty Games *(Dysfunctional Childhood)*
. (London life. Crime history.)
Journey to Moscow *(Foreigners in 1990s Soviet Union.)*
Family Ties *(Involving identical triplets and family mysteries)*
Sandie Shaw and The Millionth Marvell Cooker - *(Factory life in the 1960s)*

(Continued)

The Woman Who Drew Buildings   (Poland in 1981)
Riches of the Earth   (Early 20th Century. A Story of migrant mining families.)
Under a Brighter Sky((*Migrating from Ireland for work.)*
Land of Your Possession   (The Coventry Blitz)
A Dark Light Shining (*1930s Girl travels to France*)
Kitty Rainbow (*Early 20th Century saga,*)
Honesty's Daughter (1905 *Young woman from the North encounters America.*)
The Jagged Window   (Mid 20th C)
Gabriel Painting (*An original 'Pitman Painter*)
My Dark Eyed Girl (*Spanish Civil War*)
The Long Journey Home *(WW2 Fall of Singapore)*
The Pathfinder *(4thC AD. Wales & NE England, Celts vs Romans)*

Trilogy:

1.Kitty Rainbow 2. Children of the Storm
3. A Thirsting Land

Children's Novels

Theft
Lizza
The Real Life of Studs McGuire

Printed in Great Britain
by Amazon

57834906R00045